Tucholsky Wagner Zola Scott Sydow Freud Schlegel
Turgenev Wallace Fonatne
Twain Walther von der Vogelweide Fouqué Friedrich II. von Preußen
Weber Freiligrath Frey
Kant Ernst
Fechner Fichte Weiße Rose von Fallersleben Richthofen Frommel
Hölderlin
Engels Fielding Eichendorff Tacitus Dumas
Fehrs Faber Flaubert
Eliasberg Ebner Eschenbach
Feuerbach Maximilian I. von Habsburg Fock Zweig
Ewald Eliot Vergil
Goethe London
Mendelssohn Balzac Shakespeare Elisabeth von Österreich
Dostojewski Ganghofer
Trackl Lichtenberg Rathenau Doyle Gjellerup
Stevenson Hambruch
Mommsen Tolstoi Lenz Droste-Hülshoff
Thoma Hanrieder
von Arnim
Dach Verne Hägele Hauff Humboldt
Reuter
Karrillon Rousseau Hagen Hauptmann Gautier
Garschin
Defoe Baudelaire
Damaschke Hebbel
Descartes
Hegel Kussmaul Herder
Wolfram von Eschenbach Dickens Schopenhauer
Darwin Grimm Jerome Rilke George
Bronner Melville
Bebel
Campe Horváth Aristoteles Proust
Voltaire Federer
Bismarck Vigny Barlach Herodot
Gengenbach Heine
Storm Casanova Tersteegen Grillparzer Georgy
Chamberlain Lessing Langbein Gilm
Gryphius
Brentano Lafontaine
Claudius Schiller
Strachwitz Kralik Iffland Sokrates
Bellamy Schilling
Katharina II. von Rußland
Gerstäcker Raabe Gibbon Tschechow
Löns Hesse Hoffmann Gogol Wilde Gleim Vulpius
Luther Heym Hofmannsthal
Roth Klee Hölty Morgenstern
Heyse Klopstock Kleist Goedicke
Luxemburg Puschkin Homer Mörike
La Roche Horaz Musil
Machiavelli
Navarra Aurel Musset Kierkegaard Kraft Kraus
Lamprecht Kind Kirchhoff Hugo Moltke
Nestroy Marie de France
Laotse Ipsen Liebknecht
Nietzsche Nansen
Marx Ringelnatz
von Ossietzky Lassalle Gorki Klett Leibniz
May
vom Stein Lawrence Irving
Petalozzi
Platon Knigge
Sachs Pückler Michelangelo Kock Kafka
Poe Liebermann
Korolenko
de Sade Praetorius Mistral Zetkin

The publishing house tredition has created the series **TREDITION CLASSICS**. It contains classical literature works from over two thousand years. Most of these titles have been out of print and off the bookstore shelves for decades.

The book series is intended to preserve the cultural legacy and to promote the timeless works of classical literature. As a reader of a **TREDITION CLASSICS** book, the reader supports the mission to save many of the amazing works of world literature from oblivion.

The symbol of **TREDITION CLASSICS** is Johannes Gutenberg (1400 – 1468), the inventor of movable type printing.

With the series, tredition intends to make thousands of international literature classics available in printed format again – worldwide.

All books are available at book retailers worldwide in paperback and in hardcover. For more information please visit: www.tredition.com

tredition was established in 2006 by Sandra Latusseck and Soenke Schulz. Based in Hamburg, Germany, tredition offers publishing solutions to authors and publishing houses, combined with worldwide distribution of printed and digital book content. tredition is uniquely positioned to enable authors and publishing houses to create books on their own terms and without conventional manufacturing risks.

For more information please visit: www.tredition.com

Through St. Dunstan's to Light

James H. Rawlinson

Imprint

This book is part of the TREDITION CLASSICS series.

Author: James H. Rawlinson
Cover design: toepferschumann, Berlin (Germany)

Publisher: tredition GmbH, Hamburg (Germany)
ISBN: 978-3-8491-4731-0

www.tredition.com
www.tredition.de

CONTENTS

ILLUSTRATIONS

CHAPTER I

MY TICKET FOR BLIGHTY

In the World War, it was not only the men who went "over the top" to assault enemy positions who ran great risks. Scouts, snipers, patrols, working parties, all took their lives in their hands every time they ventured into No Man's Land, and even those who were engaged in essential work behind the lines were far from being safe from death or wounds. On the morning of June 7th, 1917, before dawn had broken, I was out with a working party. Suddenly, overhead, sounded the ominous drumming and droning of an aeroplane. It proved to be a Hun plane; the aviator had spotted us, and was speedily in touch with the battery [Pg 2] for which he was working. Fortunately for us, he had mistaken our exact position, and evidently thought we were on a road which ran towards the front line about thirty yards to our left. The enemy guns, in answer to his signals, opened up with a terrific fire, and the scenery round about was soon in a fine mess. Shells of varying calibre came thundering in our direction, throwing up, as they burst, miniature volcanoes and filling the air with dust and mud and smoke. This shellfire continued for about three-quarters of an hour, but due to the defect in the aviator's signals and our own skill in taking cover we suffered no casualties. We were congratulating ourselves that we were to pass through this ordeal uninjured, when suddenly a 5.9-inch shell fell short. It exploded almost in our midst, and I was unlucky enough to get in the way of one of the shrapnel bullets. I felt a slight sting in my right temple as though pricked by a red-hot needle—and then the world became black.

Dawn was now breaking, but night had sealed my eyes, and I could only grope my way among my comrades. I was hit about 2.30

[Pg 3] a.m., and it speaks volumes for the Medical Service that at 2 p.m. I was tucked safely in bed in a thoroughly-equipped hospital many miles from the scene of my mishap.

Willing hands tenderly dressed my wounds and led me to the foot of the ridge on which we were located. I was then placed on a stretcher, and carried up the slope to one of the narrow-gauge railways that had been run to the crest of Vimy Ridge. I was now taken to the end of what is called the Y Road, and thence borne to one of the ambulances which are always in waiting there, grim reminders of the work in hand.

My first impression of my ambulance driver was that I had fallen into the hands of a Good Samaritan. He was most solicitous about the welfare of the "head-case," and kept showering me with questions, such as: "Are you comfortable, Mac?" (everyone in the Canadian Corps was "Mac" to the stranger). "Tell me if I am driving too fast for you; you know, the roads are a little lumpy round here." I didn't know it, but I was quickly to become aware of the fact. His words and his driving did not harmonize; [Pg 4] if he missed a single shell-hole in the wide stretch of France through which he drove, it was not his fault. I shall never forget the agony of that drive; but at length, bruised and shaken, I arrived at the Casualty Clearing Station at—but, no, I will not mention its name; some of my readers may know the men who were there at the time of my arrival, and there is pain enough in the world without unnecessarily adding to the total. At the Clearing Station I learned two things: First, that all the best souvenirs of the war are in the possession of men who seldom or never saw the front line; and, secondly, the real meaning, so far as the wounded "Tommy" is concerned, of the letters R.A.M.C. The official records say they stand for the Royal Army Medical Corps; but ask the men who have passed through the hands of the Corps. They'll tell you with picturesque vehemence, and there will be nothing Royal or Medical in their answer. For my own poor part, here's hoping that the thirty-eight francs that disappeared from my pockets while in their hands did some good somewhere. But I [Pg 5] sadly wanted that money while in the hospital at Boulogne to satisfy a craving I had for oranges. Perhaps the beer or *eau de vie* that it no doubt purchased did more good than the oranges would have done me. Again, let us hope so!

From the Casualty Clearing Station I was taken to the hospital at St. Omer, which was later to be laid flat by Hun air raids. And here, for the first time, I realized the full weight of the calamity that had overtaken me, and what being "windy" really meant. I was first visited by the M.O., who removed my bandage and had my head skilfully dressed; after him came a priest of the Church to which I belonged, who administered to me the rites of the Church; then followed the assistant matron, who endeavoured to cheer me up by asking if I wished to have any letters written home. Before my inward eyes there began to flash visions of a newspaper notice: "Died of wounds." But although a bit alarmed, more by the attentions shown me than by my physical condition, the thought of pegging-out never seriously entered my mind. [Pg 6]

I spent four days at the hospital at St. Omer, and was then transferred to Boulogne, together with a New Zealand sergeant who was in the same plight as myself, and whom I later had the pleasure of meeting under more favourable and happier conditions at dear old St. Dunstan's. At Boulogne, I was given a thorough examination, and the doctors concluded that an absolutely useless member of the body was an unnecessary burden to the bearer, and so they removed what remained of my left eye. I was still vainly hoping that my right eye, which was remote from my wound, might recover its sight; but as the days crept by while the blackness of night hung about me I grew alarmed, and one day I asked the O.C. hospital why he was constantly lifting up my right eyelid. Truth to tell, I was scared stiff with the thought that they were contemplating removing my remaining eye, but I gave no outward sign of my fear. No matter how "windy" one is, it would never do to let the other fellow know it, at least not while you are wearing the uniform of the Canadians. I, therefore, quickly followed my first question with the [Pg 7] inquiry if he thought he might yet get some daylight into my right eye. "When?" he questioned. And, still clinging to the hope that I was not to be forever in the dark, I replied, "In five, ten, fifteen, twenty-five years; any time, so long as I get some light." In answer, he merely patted me on the shoulder, saying: "Never mind, things are not always quite so bad as they look." Then he moved away from my cot, and a moment later I heard him talking in undertones to another officer. This officer, whom he now brought to my bedside, proved to be Captain Towse, the bravest man it has ever been my privilege to meet, and while I was up the line I met many brave men who, where duty called, counted life not at a pin's fee.

Captain Towse is a double V.C. It is hard enough to get the Cross itself, and there are few men who dare even to dream of a bar to it. I was now in personal touch with a man who, in distant Africa, during the Great Boer War, with both eyes shot away, had gallantly stood firm, urging his men to the charge. He came to my bedside [Pg 8] with a cheery: "Good morning, Canada! How is the boy this morning?" My answer was the usual one of the boys in France: "Jakealoo!" Then he pointedly asked me a question that set me wondering at its purport.

"You are a soldier, are you not, Canada?"

I replied with a somewhat mournful: "Well, I was one time, but I can't say much as to the truth of that now."

Then he hit me harder than any Hun shell could hit a man. He snapped out in a voice penetrating, yet with a cheery ring to it: "Well, you are blind, and for life. How do you like it?"

For about five seconds (it was no longer) the night that sealed my eyes seemed to clutch my soul. I was for the moment "down and out"; but I braced my spirits in the presence of this dominating man. I would show him how a Canadian soldier could bear misfortune. So I gathered myself together as best I could under the circumstances; swore just a little to ease my nervous strain, and replied: "That's a hell of a thing to tell a guy." [Pg 9]

Then came words that rolled a mighty load from heart and brain. Captain Towse praised my soldierly bearing under misfortune, and praise from this blind double V.C. meant much. He had been sorely smitten at a time when there was no St. Dunstan's, no Sir Arthur Pearson, to make his blindness into just a handicap, instead of what it nearly always was before the days of St. Dunstan's, an unparalleled affliction. But Captain Towse beat blindness, and did it, for the most part, alone.

Now the cruel fact had to be faced; the only world I would see henceforth would be that conjured up by the imagination from memories of the past. Then the difficulties of the future crowded upon me. Even if I were not to see as other people do I should still have to eat; and dinners do not grow by the roadside, and if they did I could not see to pick them up.

"Well, Jim," I said to myself, "you are in a fine fix; what are you going to do to get those three square meals a day that you were accustomed to in civil life?" Then I began to wonder what particular street and [Pg 10] what street corner in old Toronto would be best suited for selling matches, bootlaces, pencils, and postcards. While in this vein, I conjured up visions of cold, grey days, days when customers did not appear, and imagined myself led home at night without having enough to buy even a meal. My humour suggested strolling along the roadside singing doleful songs. I even chose a song, "The Blind Boy," by the late W. G. Chirgwin, on which I might try my voice.

All this passed through my mind while Captain Towse was still standing by my cot.

I was suddenly startled from my gruesome speculations by the captain asking me if I had made up my mind to go to St. Dunstan's. I had to confess that I did not know the place, where it was, or what it was for. Then he told me that he wished to take down some particulars regarding me. He wanted to know my full name, regimental number, when I was hit, where I received my wound, who was my next of kin, and many other particulars, all of which I, at that time, thought a most unnecessary and foolish proceeding. [Pg 11]

While the Captain was questioning me, I heard a rapid, clicking sound following each of my answers. The noise fascinated me, and after a brief time I made bold to ask him what it was. The answer fairly staggered me.

"It's a Braille machine," he replied. "I am writing down your answers."

I knew he was blind—blinder than any bat; and, in my ignorance, I asked him, in an irritated voice, if he thought that it was fair to try "to kid" a man who had just been told that he would never again have the use of his eyes. He uttered no word, but I had a feeling that a smile was playing on his lips; and the next moment the machine he had been operating was placed in my hands. He then began patiently to explain its use, and what a moment before had seemed an utter impossibility I realized to be a fact. Although the blind could not see, they at least had it in their power to put down their thoughts without the aid of a second party; and, not only that, the world of knowledge was no longer a sealed book—they could read as well as write. The eye had been [Pg 12] accustomed to carry the printed word to the brain; now the finger tips could take the place of eyes. I now recalled that I had seen a blind man sitting at a street corner, running his fingers over the pages of a big book; but I had paid no heed to it, thinking it merely a fake performance to gain sympathy from the public. I told this to Captain Towse, and he replied kindly that I should soon learn much greater things about the blind. At St. Dunstan's, he said, there were about three hundred men, all more or less sightless, making baskets, mats, hammocks, nets, bags, and dozens of other useful articles, mending boots, doing carpentry, learning the poultry business, fitting themselves for massage work, and, what seemed to me most incredible, taking up stenography as an occupation.

The Boot-Repairing Workshop

Men—men who could not see as did other men, were doing these things; straightway, the old street corner, the selling of matches and shoelaces, the street strolling singing in a cracked voice while twanging some tuneless instrument, vanished. Other men had risen above this crowning infirmity; why could not [Pg 13] I. Boulogne and this meeting with Captain Towse had saved me. Gloom vanished, for the moment at any rate, and my whole being was animated by a great resolve—the resolve to win in the battle of life, even though I had to fight against fearful odds. [Pg 14]

CHAPTER II

IN BLIGHTY

It was with a sense of relief that, shortly after this, I received word that I was to be sent to England. To me, it was the promised land, in which I was to be fitted to take my place as a useful, independent member of society. The trip to Dover was pleasant and exhilarating; the run to London a bit tedious. But an incident that occurred on my arrival at Charing Cross Station touched my heart as has nothing else in my life, and my misfortune seemed, for the moment, almost a blessing; it taught me that hearts beat right and true, and that about me were men and women eager to cheer me on as I played the game of life.

It was just one of London's flower-girls, one of the women who religiously meet the hospital trains and shower on the wounded soldiers the flowers they have not sold—flowers, no doubt, held back from sale in [Pg 15] most cases for this charitable purpose. When the attendants were moving me from the train and placing me on a stretcher, I was gently touched, and a large bunch of roses placed in my hand. The act was accompanied by the words: "'Ere ye are, Tommy. These 'ere roses will 'elp to liven things up a bit when yer gets in the 'ospital. Good luck to you, matey; may yer soon get better." The voice was harsh and unmusical. Grammar and accent showed that it had been trained in the slums; but the kindly act, the sympathetic words, touched my soul.

The act was much to me, but the flowers were nothing. In answer to the girl's good wishes, I replied that I did not see as well as I used to, and that my power of enjoying the perfume of flowers had also been taken from me; perhaps there were some other wounded boys who could appreciate the beauty and scent of the flowers better than I could, and she had better put them on one of their stretchers. But she left them with me, and, in a voice in which I could detect a tear, said: [Pg 16] —

"Well, matey, if yer can't see, yer can feel. Let's give yer a kiss."

I nodded assent, and then I received the first kiss from a woman's lips that I had had since I left home—and then she passed away, but the memory of that kiss remains, and will remain while life lasts.

I was now taken to St. George's Hospital, and from there to No. 2 London General Hospital (old St. Mark's College), Chelsea. In this institution I met for the first time one of the geniuses of the present age, a man who spent his life working not with clay or marble, or wood or metal, but with human beings, taking the derelicts of life and moulding them into useful vessels—Sir Arthur Pearson, a true miracle worker, a man who has given the equivalent of eyes to hundreds of blind people, who has enabled many men who felt themselves down and out to face life's battle bravely, teaching them to look upon their affliction as nothing more than a petty handicap. A few years ago, as everyone knows, Sir Arthur was one of the leading journalists and publishers in the British Empire, the true founder of Imperial [Pg 17] journalism. At the summit of his career, while still a comparatively young man, he was smitten with blindness. He would not let a thing like that beat him; he conquered blindness, and set himself to help others to conquer it. He soon became the leading spirit in the education of the blind in Great Britain, and, despite his handicap, was elected President of the National Institute for the Blind, and was the guiding star in many organizations established to aid the sightless. When war broke out his success as an organizer, his power as a teacher, caused the authorities to choose him to look after the blinded of the Army and Navy.

Sir

Arthur Pearson

My meeting with Sir Arthur occurred in the following manner. The ward door was open—I knew that by the gentle breeze that swept across my cot. Suddenly, from the direction of the door, a cheery voice exclaimed: "Are any new men here? Where's Rawlinson?"

I answered: "Right here, sir! But who are you?"

"Well, Rawlinson, and how are you getting along? When do they figure on letting you [Pg 18] get away from here? You know, we are waiting for you at St. Dunstan's."

I knew then that the man standing by my cot was the famous Sir Arthur. I shook hands with him, and thanked him for his kindly interest in asking about me. I offered him the chair that always stands beside the hospital bed. He must have heard me moving some objects I had placed on it, in order to have them within reach of my hands.

"Never mind the chair," he said. "Just sit up a bit; there is room enough on the bed for both of us. Have you got a cigarette to give a fellow?"

I apologized, saying that I had only — — — —, and that I didn't think he would care to smoke them.

"Do you smoke them?" he questioned. "If they're good enough for you to smoke, they're good enough for me."

That set me right at my ease. I was in the presence of a knight; but he was first and last a *man*. Straight to the point he went. He never puts a man through that bugbear of the soldier, a host of seemingly inconsequential questions; he has the particu [Pg 19] lars of each man who is likely to come under his direction long before he visits him.

"Have you," he said, "made up your mind to join our happy band at St. Dunstan's. There's lots of room up there for you, and we want you."

Just here I would remark that No. 2 General was a sort of preparatory school for St. Dunstan's. The adjutant from one of the St. Dunstan's establishments, either the House, College, or Bungalow, came to read the newspapers and talk with the men who were to study under him. So we had by this means picked up much information about Sir Arthur, and knew the man even before meeting him; but the being conjured up by our imagination fell far short of the real man. He did not come to your bedside commiserating with you over your misfortune. He was totally unlike the average visitor, whose one aim seemed to be to impress on you some appropriate — often most inappropriate, considering your condition — text of scripture. Well, he was with me, and we talked and smoked, the knight and the private soldier, both blind, but both completely ignoring the fact. Dur [Pg 20] ing our talk darkness seemed to vanish, and I saw a great light — the battle could be won, and I would win it. After that conference, I knew full well that I should not be a burden upon anybody, sightless though I was.

Up to this time my idea of a blind man was just what is or was that of the average sighted person — a man groping his way about the streets or standing at some conspicuous corner with a card hanging on his breast telling the world that he could not see; a cup to hold the coppers that the sympathetic public would drop into it; and last, but not least, a faithful little dog, his friend and guide. During the first days of my blindness I often wondered where I was going to get a suitable pup.

While at No. 2 London General, preparation for my future work went on. As soon as I was able to get out of bed, I was taken once each week to St. Dunstan's to talk with other men in residence there — a species of initiation. While in hospital, too, as soon as we were able to work a little, we were given the rudiments of Braille. This was not compulsory; and if we wished to yield to [Pg 21] fate and sit with hands idly folded we were at liberty to do so. But the majority of the men were eager for occupation of any kind.

Lying in bed or sitting on a hospital chair, unable to see the objects about you, there is a danger of deep depression being occasioned by melancholy brooding. To prevent this, the V.A.D.'s who worked in the St. Dunstan's Ward saw to it that the men were not left too much to themselves, and kindly attention kept me from becoming morbid while waiting for my exchange to St. Dunstan's.

As I was a Canadian, I had to go down to the Canadian Hospital to receive my final Board—just a matter of that child of the devil, red-tape. August 13th saw me on my way to Regent's Park, where St. Dunstan's is situated. My heart leaped within me; I was going to have first-hand knowledge of the marvellous things about which I had heard. I was going to learn things that would put me out of the stick, tin-cup, card-around-my-neck, and little-dog class. Thirteen may be an unlucky number, but that 13th of August was, notwithstanding my blindness, the be [Pg 22] ginning of the happiest year of my life since I left my mother's home.

On my way to St. Dunstan's, I journeyed from the Marble Arch to Orchard Street, then by bus up Orchard Street, Upper Baker and Baker Streets, right past Marylebone, on the right of which stands Madame Tussaud's famous Wax-Works, and on to Baker Street tube. Just past the tube is Clarence Gate, one of the entrances to Regent's Park. Entering the grounds, we followed the park rails until we came to two white stone pillars. I have painful recollections of these pillars. For the first two weeks after my arrival at St. Dunstan's I made their acquaintance frequently, and in no pleasant manner. I was anxious to find my way about without assistance, and those pillars always seemed to stand in my way. Head, shoulders, and shins all bumped into them. They would meet me even if I walked in the broad roadway. And they were hard, very hard. They were at first a pair of veritable ogres, but in the end I conquered them, and could walk by them with a jaunty air, whistling a tune of defiance. [Pg 23]

CHAPTER III

AT ST. DUNSTAN'S

When I arrived at St. Dunstan's, the place was practically deserted. The summer holidays were on, and all the men were away, either at their homes in the British Isles or at one of the annexes of St. Dunstan's. Sir Arthur sees to it that no man goes without his vacation. Torquay and Brighton were within easy reach, and at these seaside resorts there were rest homes for the St. Dunstan's men. Since that time, so greatly has the attendance increased, it has been found necessary to open other vacation resorts. It is to these places that the sightless Colonials go. When the boys got back, work began in earnest.

I have been speaking of St. Dunstan's; it is now fitting that I give a description of this Mecca of the sightless, or, as we say, of those who do not see quite as well as other people. A hostel for the training of those having [Pg 24] defective sight suggests a barrack-like structure with whitewashed walls, board forms for the accommodation of the students, and the rudest of furniture. What need is there of the beautiful for those who are without eyes, or who have eyes that see not? But the blind have a keen appreciation of the beautiful, and ample provision has been made by the founders of St. Dunstan's for satisfying the aesthetic craving of the students.

St. Dunstan's: The House

St. Dunstan's stands on one of the largest estates in the city of London. It is surpassed in size only by the Royal Palace of Buckingham. The grounds are over sixteen acres in extent, and it has one of the most beautiful lawns in the United Kingdom. The House belongs to Mr. Otto Kahn, an American financier, who played an important part in bringing the United States to the side of the Allies. When Sir Arthur Pearson started out on his big drive in the interests of the soldiers and sailors who might be deprived of their sight in the Great World War, Mr. Kahn generously laid the whole of this magnificent estate at his disposal. The House itself is one of the most famous in the United [Pg 25] Kingdom. In the days when it was the property of Lord Londesborough, it was often the scene of royal gatherings. The Kaiser visited it so frequently that the people in the vicinity began to look upon his coming as a matter of course. Entering the gate to the left, the first object to meet the eye is the lodge-keeper's house, a picturesque, rose-embowered structure. Then comes the lawn, a wide stretch of velvety turf, cool and restful. The approach to the House itself is through an avenue of mulberry trees, well intermingled with lime. In the summer season the air is filled with the scent of flowers, welling forth from roses, yellow jasmine, and pink almond blossoms. Entering the building by the main entrance, to the left of the hallway the visitor sees the office of Sir Arthur and those of his staff, who, under the supervision of the chief, control the hostel. At either side of the hallway are two magnificent chairs, one of which was the favourite seat of Edward the Peacemaker, and the other that of Kaiser Wilhelm II., the German War Lord. Passing through the hallway, the lounge room is reached, and [Pg 26] a little farther the outer lounge, formerly Lord Londesborough's ballroom, where are staged the charming concerts for which the House is famous.

But St. Dunstan's is not a mere resthouse. It is essentially a humming hive of industry, an educational institution where there is something for everyone to learn. Whether a man can see or not, he can here find occupation for his hands and mind. After all, we do not *see* with our *eyes*; they merely carry sights to the seeing brain, and the hands, and even feet, can perform the same duties, only in a different way. Teachers were many and willing. And here I should like to record the fact that no one can teach the blind quite as well as the other fellow who is also sightless. I know whereof I speak, for I have been piloted around localities by people who could see and also by people whose "eyesight was not as good as it once was." This last expression is borrowed from Sir Arthur, who always speaks of his sightless boys as: "The boys whose eyesight is not quite as good as it once was."

About a week after the boys had returned [Pg 27] from their vacation, I had a chance to visit the workshops. What a hive of industry these same workshops are! Go there, you men and women blessed with sight, and see for yourselves what your sightless brother is doing in the way of making himself over again, bringing into play his latent powers, and turning what seemed to be a worthless creature, a burden to himself and humanity, into the only asset—a producer—that is worth while to any country. The obstacles he faces at the beginning seem unsurmountable; but at St. Dunstan's the spirit of the place grips him and the word "cannot" disappears from his dictionary. But at first he has much to unlearn. All his old methods of work have to be forgotten. He is, in a sense, a child again, born the day his sight was taken from him. But though his sight is lost, if he is the right sort, the greatest asset a man possesses can never be taken from him—his spirit, his determination never to be a burden on others; his feeling, his knowledge that what others have done he can do. His confidence in his ability to make good, his spirit of independence — he still has these, and they enable [Pg 28] him to win greater victories than any he might have achieved in battle, victories over that terror of the sighted — blindness.

Those of us who claim St. Dunstan's as our *Alma Mater* are often told that we can talk of nothing but the place and the treatment we received there. Our answer is: Out of the abundance of the heart the mouth speaketh. She took us up when we were in the depths and remade us into *men*; she taught us to be real producers; she made it possible for us to take our place in the ranks of the earners — in fact, all that we know and all that we are we owe to her. There is only one point on which Sir Arthur and his boys disagree. Sir Arthur claims that it was the boys who made St. Dunstan's; the boys maintain that St. Dunstan's made the men. While I was in residence there, there were about five hundred and fifty men undergoing instruction, and yet St. Dunstan's carried on smoothly and serenely without the slightest vestige of discipline in the ordinary sense of the word. Only two per cent. of those who passed through the institution failed to make good. What other educa [Pg 29] tional establishment can boast such a record? And yet nothing was compulsory except sobriety.

I was at St. Dunstan's for sixteen months, and as my case was typical I cannot do better, in order to give a detailed account of the work there, than relate my own experiences. When I was ready to begin work, I went before the Adjutant and arranged what courses I would take up. Times for classes were fixed, teachers named, and everything done to enable me to begin my training for the battle of life. I was, as it were, a child again, about to enter school for the second time, but under vastly different conditions from my first entrance, about a quarter of a century before. Braille and typewriting were taken up as a matter of course. Braille is taught to enable the sightless to read for themselves, and typewriting in order that it will not be so hard on their friends, as it is much easier for the blind to learn to typewrite than it is for the sighted to learn to read Braille. It took me four months to master Braille, but I passed my typewriting test in less than three weeks. I was pleased with my achieve [Pg 30] ment in respect to the latter, as I had determined to take up stenography and typewriting as a profession. There was an added incentive for the students to take up typewriting, for Sir Arthur, the most generous of men, presents each of his boys with a typewriter when he is leaving St. Dunstan's.

The occupations were varied, and in my early days as a student, my greatest pleasure was to visit the various rooms where workers were engaged at different callings. Here some were repairing shoes, and humming ditties happily as they worked; now the rustling and crackling told me that I was in the presence of men making baskets and mats; again, the sound of hammers driving home nails and of planes made me aware that I was among carpenters. In addition to these trades, men were at work studying poultry-keeping, and taking courses in massage work. At first I viewed all this from the attitude of the sighted, and it seemed to me an unparalleled miracle; but after a time I took it all as a matter of course.

The Carpenter Shop

The stenographic and massage courses take the longest time; but at St. Dunstan's there is [Pg 31] no time limit set for any course. If proficiency is not achieved in one month or six months, the student

26

can keep doggedly at it for a longer period. St. Dunstan's is a home until proficiency in the chosen calling is achieved. "Grow proficient" was Sir Arthur's demand of his boys; and with few exceptions they stuck at it till he was satisfied.

The time of actual work for each man was about three and a half hours per day. From this it will be seen that it was not all work at St. Dunstan's. While the main purpose of the institution is to make producers of men with a serious handicap, another great aim is to brighten their lives and create in them that buoyant spirit — the *moral* of life — that is half the battle. [Pg 32]

CHAPTER IV

BRAILLE

I have often been asked, "What is Braille? Is it raised letters?" Braille was originated by a Frenchman named Louis Braille, in 1829, and, with a few trifling changes, stands to-day as it left the hands of its inventor. The base of the system consists of six raised dots enclosed in what is called a cell, thus —

The dots are numbered as follows: left-hand dots, 1, 3, 5; right-hand, 2, 4, 6. For reading purposes the dots are arranged in cells corresponding to the base cell, each cell being a letter or contraction. In Grade II Braille, there are in all eighty-two word and letter signs. The letters of the alphabet [Pg 33] are as follows:

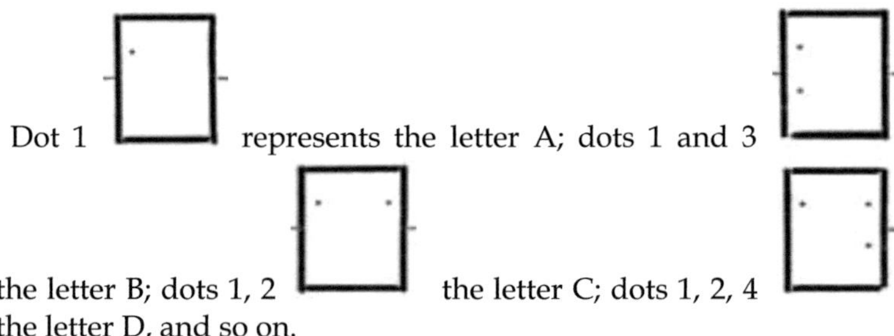

Dot 1 represents the letter A; dots 1 and 3 the letter B; dots 1, 2 the letter C; dots 1, 2, 4 the letter D, and so on.

The arrangement of the dots in the cell gives not only all the letters of the alphabet, but signs that stand for words and phrases as well.

I began the study of Braille with Miss Gilles, a New Zealand lady, as my instructor, while I was at St. Mark's Hospital. I was first given a wooden box full of holes. Into these holes my teacher showed me how to put nails with large heads, the nails being placed in cells to correspond with the Braille alphabet. After I had succeeded in grasping the principle of Braille by means of the nails—which, by the way, I frequently jabbed into my fingers instead of into the holes—I was given a card with the alphabet on it. At [Pg 34] first the dots seemed without form and void; and when I was asked what numbers I felt, I did wish for my eyes, as I was utterly unable to convey to my brain the letter under my fingers. The hardest part of Braille for the beginner is not in getting it into the head, but in getting the fingers to take the place of eyes. But it is only necessary to persevere to get the proper, illuminating "touch" into the finger tips. The men made sightless in the war were in most cases confronted with grave difficulties. Their hands were hardened by toil, and their fingers calloused by work in the trenches. One of my comrades, when given his Braille card, struggled over it for a time, and then exclaimed: "I wish they'd leave this card out in the rain till the dots swelled to the size of door-knobs; then I might be able to read it."

The Braille Room

Before I left St. Mark's I had mastered the first ten letters of the alphabet; but I was soon to learn that if one does not keep at it, "touch" will be lost. After leaving St. Mark's, I spent three idle weeks at Folkestone. As a result, when I arrived at St. Dunstan's I had to begin my Braille all over [Pg 35] again. My teacher at St. Dunstan's, Miss Wineberg, proved herself as patient as was Miss Gilles; but patience is a characteristic virtue of all the women who instructed the sightless boys in the Braille Room, and among them were some of the best-known ladies in England, four having titles. These teachers sit for hours making men "stick it," in many cases against their will, until they have mastered the mystery of correctly judging the number and arrangement of dots under the finger tip. The theory of Braille can be grasped in six weeks by the average student; but it takes from four to six months to so cultivate touch as to make the fingers readily take the place of eyes. After the reading of Braille has been mastered, writing it, an even more difficult operation, is taken up. When I had satisfactorily passed my test in both reading and writing, I entered that holy of holies, the Shorthand Room. The four teachers in this room are all blind. Our teacher was Corporal Charles McIntosh, who had lost both his eyes and his right leg while with the Gallipoli Expeditionary Force. I have stated that there are eighty-two signs [Pg 36] in Grade II Braille; but Braille shorthand contains six hundred and eighty word and letter signs that have to be committed to memory. A herculean task was before me, but by dogged effort on my part and patience on the part of my instructor, I succeeded so well that in a few weeks I was able to take shorthand notes as speedily as the average sighted stenographer. Meanwhile, I had been diligently at work at my typewriting, and under the kindly instruction of Miss Dorothy Charles Dickens, a granddaughter of the great novelist, I had soon acquired sufficient speed and accuracy to qualify for work. [Pg 37]

CHAPTER V

THE SPIRIT OF ST. DUNSTAN's

To give an adequate account of the work done at St. Dunstan's, and of the spirit of the place, it is necessary to touch upon the personnel of the hostel. I have already dwelt at some length on the patient self-sacrifice of the teachers of Braille: the spirit they display animates the entire staff. The work of the V.A.D.'s is beyond praise. Very few of these noble women actually live on the premises; most of them live in annexes provided for them by the St. Dunstan's management. What they do, what they endure, can best be comprehended by following them through a day's work.

They rise at 6 a.m., and after acting as their own housemaids for their sleeping apartments, wend their way to the various houses to which they are assigned. Breakfast hour is at 7 a.m. After this meal, the real work of the day begins. At the Bungalow, where [Pg 38] I was staying, the V.A.D.'s ate at three tables; and after each meal two were told off to clear the tables. At 8 o'clock the men had their breakfast, two of the women being given the task of waiting on each table; and as they had to attend to sixteen men, all healthy specimens of humanity, some of whom had been out on the lake since early morning, getting up a voracious appetite, their work was far from light. There was, I might say just here, no shortage of food at St. Dunstan's, not even while the war was on; and we had a lingering suspicion that Sir Arthur had a "pull" with the Food Minister. At any rate, he secured us all we could eat, and of excellent variety; and there were few in London who could say as much after food was rationed. Breakfast over, the Sisters, as they are called, went to the dormitories. Each dormitory held twenty-five beds; and with these and in other ways, they were kept busy until 11.45. The dinner hour was twelve o'clock. After dinner some of the men always went for a row on the lake; and of course, they needed some one to steer the boat. A Sister was called, and she gladly [Pg 39] joined the boys. During my entire stay at the Bungalow, I never heard one grumble or complain at these calls on her time and energy. At 2 p.m., the morning Sisters went off duty, and their time was their own until six in the evening, when they again came on, and devoted themselves to the needs of the men until nine o'clock. They were allowed one afternoon a week, which afternoon began at 6 p.m.; and on this day they were on duty until this hour from six in the morning. In addition, they were granted a week-end every three months. These women did their bit during the war—and are still doing it—as truly as did the men at the front. Their work was hard, nerve-racking, and often of a disagreeable kind; and it must be remembered that many of them had never so much as dusted off their own pianos before taking up their duties at St. Dunstan's.

The matron of the Bungalow was Mrs. Craven, a sympathetic woman of heroic mould, and with a wide experience in war work. She has two South African medals, and for twelve months was matron of the hospital at Bar-le-Duc that Fritzie once [Pg 40] termed "that damned little British hospital," just eight miles behind the lines at Verdun; at a time when the Germans were exerting their utmost power to break through, and were making the destruction of hospitals and clearing stations a specialty. Mrs. Craven was every inch a soldier. The following incident admirably illustrates her character. One of the men was one day calling for a Sister just at the time that they were going off duty for the morning, and waiting to be relieved by the afternoon Sisters. The man had called three or four times at the top of his voice, "Sister! Sister! Anybody's Sister!" There was no response. The matron heard him, and rushed to his assistance. As she passed through the Lounge Room she met a Sister—a new one, by the way—who had paid no attention to the call. The matron asked her, somewhat sternly, "Did you not hear that man calling?"

"Yes, Matron; but I am off duty now."

"Off duty! If you were up the line and were going off duty, and a convoy of broken, bleeding men were being brought in, would you think that you would be justified in not [Pg 41] going to their aid because you were off duty?"

"Under such circumstances I should not think of such a thing."

"Well, I wish you to remember that there is no time here when you are off duty. While working in St. Dunstan's all the staff are on duty for twenty-four hours a day. These men have been deprived of the most precious thing God had given them while seeing to it that we women might live here in comparative safety and comfort. I am here to see to their welfare, and I intend that everyone working with me shall do the same at all seasons and all hours. Never let me hear you speak of being off duty again when a cry of distress goes up. The work here is just as important as if you were up the line. These men, although healed of their open wounds, need our aid, for the time being at any rate, to help them bear the burden that has been laid upon them."

Mrs. Craven was a veritable mother to all who came under her care, and the boys showed their appreciation of her services when she was "called up" by the War Office to take charge at one of the largest hospitals in England. [Pg 42]

The matron of the House, known to all as "Sister Pat," was compelled to retire from her position on account of a breakdown in health. When she was leaving, the boys presented her with a trifling gift as a mark of their esteem, and to keep them green in her memory. But no gift was needed for that. As she accepted the present, she said: "Boys, Sister Pat will come back to you. She cannot leave her boys for ever. I will come back to you if you will have me, if it is only to clean your boots." Her place in the heart of her boys will never be filled.

Then there was Captain McMahon, adjutant at the Bungalow. The captain had lost a leg in the South African War. The operation had not been a success, and the "Skipper," as we affectionately called him, put in many painful hours. To my own knowledge, on one occasion, he endured extreme suffering for thirty-six hours at a stretch. It was clear to all that a second operation was needed. One day, while in his office, I asked him why he did not go to a hospital and have another amputation. My remark was an innocent one, but I was quickly made to regret it. [Pg 43]

"Rawlinson," he replied, "I did not think you would ask me such a question."

"Why?" I continued.

"Why!" he snapped back. "Don't you know that there are still hundreds of boys coming down the line wounded and broken?"

"Yes," I answered. "But why should that stop you?"

Then I got it. "Jim," he said, "there might be one of those boys that would require the bed that I occupied, and my being there might necessitate that lad having to go to one of the hospitals perhaps right in the north of England. No, Jim, I will wait till all of them have been set on their feet again before I make application for a bed in one of the London hospitals."

And so Captain McMahon heroically continued to bear his suffering rather than keep one of the derelicts from France out of a bed. Next to Sir Arthur Pearson, he was dearest to the men in the Bungalow. They loved him, and there was not one of the two hundred and fifty men there who would not gladly have allowed him to walk over his body if it would be for his good. The [Pg 44] "Skipper" was a Man, a man's man, a father to all of us, whom it was good to know. When the boys were worried they took their troubles to him. He made all their worries his own, and it was surprising what a big load of care he could carry.

Mrs. Craven, "Sister Pat," and Captain McMahon were leaders in the life at St. Dunstan's. But the whole place was animated with the same spirit that inspired them; the spirit that manifested itself in its fulness in Sir Arthur Pearson, and in a lesser degree in every student. It made all the boys workers, and created in them the desire to help others, to make the world a little better for their being in it, even if they had to work under a handicap. [Pg 45]

CHAPTER VI

AIR RAIDS

When I left the shores of France I thought I was permanently out of danger from the death-dealing missiles of the enemy; not that I cared much then; I had received such a blow that I should not greatly have regretted a stroke that would have ended my earthly career. But the arm of Germany was long, the ingenuity of the War Lords great; by means of their magnificent submarines they had carried the war to the shores of England, so by their superb air force they were to bring it to the heart of London; indeed, by their Zeppelins, those crowning failures of their efficiency, they had already done that.

I had been in London but a short time when, on Saturday, July 21st, 1917, I had my first experience of an air raid in a crowded city. At the time I was in St. Mark's Hospital, undergoing my preliminary training for St. Dunstan's, at the moment in the [Pg 46] ward receiving instruction in Braille. Shortly before noon some one entered the room and exclaimed jubilantly that a vast flock of aeroplanes, estimated at from thirty to sixty, were manœuvring at a great height in battle formation over the city, and we were congratulating ourselves that the War Office had at length aroused itself and was demonstrating its ability to cope with any attack by heavier-than-air machines that the enemy might send over. As we listened to the news and longed for our eyes that we might have a sight of this spectacle, the thunderous report of a bursting bomb undeceived us. These planes were not marked with the friendly tricoloured circles, but with the ominous cross. There were cries of terror, a hurrying of feet, a near panic as bomb succeeded bomb. Many of us had been disciplined to war conditions, had dodged bombs at the Somme and Vimy Ridge, dodged them when shrapnel was spraying about us and machine-gun and rifle bullets made the air hiss on every side; but this attack in the heart of a great city was not without its terrifying aspect. After having escaped death on the [Pg 47] battle-field, it would be horrible to have to meet it in the tumbling ruins of a crushed building. But we faced the situation stoically. London and its suburbs had over 7,000,000 people, and, by the theory of chances, we concluded that we were not likely to be hit.

This was the first Hun aeroplane success over London, the only one in which he accomplished anything of value from a military point of view, one bomb knocking a corner off the General Post Office, St. Martin's in the Field, and almost disrupting the whole of the telegraph system that was carrying messages to and from military headquarters. There was, of course, the usual slaughter of defenceless women and children, deeds that the Hun hoped would terrorize England, lower the *moral* of her people, and keep a large army within the island for home defence. How little he knew the British race! The deplorable thing in connection with the raid was that while it was in progress there was not a single machine in the air combatting the attackers, and not an anti-aircraft gun in action. The War Office [Pg 48] needed to be roused from its slumbers. It was; and when the next raiders came over they had a warm reception.

My next experience was in the open. One day I was walking through London's streets when the approach of a raiding force was announced. Shelters were by this time provided for the citizens, and to one of these underground bomb-proof spots, a tube, I made my way. At this time, London was largely a city of women and foreigners—at least so it seemed to me. I had evidently hit upon a shelter of a most cosmopolitan character. The place was packed with a frightened mob, trembling and groaning with terror, and expressing their fears in many tongues utterly unknown to me. The air was stifling with that distinctive odour that seems to emanate from the great unwashed; in this case garlic seemed to be the prevailing perfume. It was a mixed crowd, however, and women in silks rubbed shoulders with women in tattered gowns, all moved by the one thought—self-preservation. Most of them, I judged by their cries and gasps, were almost insane with terror. But there were heroines [Pg 49] among them. Two women near me were holding an animated conversation.

"Say," said one, "ain't it time that this war wuz over? Why don't they stop? I haven't been in bed to stay for over six nights, and I'm getting tired of it all."

The answer told the real spirit of the average British woman, a spirit that was doing much to win the war.

"Liza," replied the first speaker's companion, in a somewhat indignant voice, "Bill's over there, ain't 'e? 'E's tryin' to stop that — — blighter from treatin' us like 'e did the women of Belgium and France. 'E's gettin' this every day, and still smiles and sticks it. Yer can't git me to say stop it. Carry on is my motter till the — — Hun is slugged out of existence."

This rough, humble Cockney woman displayed the same spirit that was being shown by the Women's Army Auxiliary Corps in France. The girls of this corps took it upon themselves to do the work that was being done by men who thought themselves permanently installed in bomb-proof jobs. What is more, they did it well. Take this one instance. [Pg 50] During the German drive of 1918, some of these girls were working in canteens a short distance behind the front line. As the Germans swept forward with irresistible might, and had almost reached the camps and billets where the W.A.A.C.'s were, the girls were ordered to leave the danger zone in motor lorries. They refused, saying: "Those waggons can be used to carry wounded men back; we can walk." And walk they did; slinging their packs on their backs and marching nineteen miles over rough, muddy roads. But not all of them; some of the boldest stayed behind to see that the boys got hot tea or coffee to revive their tired, in most cases, wounded and broken bodies. Their courage brought them under shell-fire; but they carried on dauntlessly. During my last days in London, when I was singing at one of their hostels, I met four of these women, each of whom had lost a leg, and one was proudly wearing a Military Medal.

The woman of the tube and the refined W.A.A.C.'s were "sisters under the skin." Had the former had her way, she would have been at Bill's side, handing him cartridges while he potted the enemy. [Pg 51]

While I was at the Bungalow, we had a somewhat thrilling experience from air raids. In September, 1917, the raiders were exceptionally bold, and during the first ten days of the month visited London no fewer than eight times. Night after night we were roused by the whistling of sirens and the bursting of maroons, thin shells that made a big noise, warning all that an air raid was in progress, and giving pedestrians and others a chance to take shelter from enemy bombs and the shrapnel of the anti-aircraft guns, the latter even a greater menace to those in the open than the former. On one of these nights I, with two Canadian chums, sightless like myself, had just entered the Bungalow when the maroons began to explode and the whistles to shriek. Bed was out of the question. Besides, the matron, Mrs. Craven, would be up on the instant to look after her boys. True to form, the matron appeared, and we drew up one of the Davenports in front of a cheerful grate fire.

"Are all you boys feeling right?" asked the matron.

Before we had time to answer, the anti [Pg 52] -aircraft guns opened up their barrage. They seemed to be shooting right over the Bungalow, for pieces of shrapnel clattered on the roof like great hailstones. One piece, about a pound in weight, smashed through the roof and into the matron's room. As we sat there, overhead we could hear the angry droning of the Hun planes and the whistling rush of the dropping bombs, each moment expecting one to crash among us. A bomb that dropped near by, in St. John's Wood, sounded as it if were going to pay us a visit, and I nervously remarked: "This one is ours, Matron!"

"Well, Rawlinson," she replied, without a quiver in her voice, "we are still soldiers, you know, and if it comes, what better could we ask than a soldier's death."

That night four bombs dropped in the grounds within a radius of four hundred yards, but fortunately none of them did any material damage.

On another night we were being entertained at one of the delightful concerts arranged for us by the staff. The concert was at its height when the guns opened up. Our entertainers suggested stopping the per [Pg 53] formance, but we objected to having such a trifling matter as an air raid interfere with our fun, and the concert went merrily on, and before it was over the Huns were beating it for home, chased by daring British aviators.

On several occasions the raiders hove in sight after the inmates of the Bungalow were all in bed. But Sir Arthur had seen to it that we should be warned in time, so that in case we received a direct hit we should not be caught like rats in a trap. News of the approaching raiders was sent in by the telephone simultaneously with its receipt by the police authorities, and one of the orderlies on watch visited the rooms and roused the men, instructing any who so wished to take refuge in the shrapnel-proof cellars over at the House. Needless to say, none of the boys rushed for shelter — not from our ward, at any rate. We either got up and dressed to enjoy the thrill of listening to the droning planes, bursting bombs, and clattering shrapnel, or lay in bed, quietly taking the whole matter with philosophical indifference. The danger signal came as soon as the raiders crossed the East Coast, and then all was [Pg 54] hubbub and excitement in London until the "all clear" was sounded by that gallant little — little in body, but big in heart — band of boys known as the Boy Scouts, who were posted at every police station.

No doubt many of us felt a bit "windy" during these raids, but in the presence of the other fellow we would not show it. Our buildings and grounds, right in the heart of London, were most conspicuous; and, besides, Regent's Park was not without its military importance, for in it were kept the aerodrome stores. Its lake and the canal which runs between it and the Zoo, made it a shining mark for the Hun bombers. But we stood our ground fearlessly through all these raids, listening to the din of this aerial warfare, awed not so much by the explosions as by the bedlam created in the Zoo, where, as soon as a raid was on, the lions roared, elephants madly trumpeted, monkeys chattered, parrots shrieked, and wolves howled dismally. [Pg 55]

CHAPTER VII

ROYAL VISITORS

St. Dunstan's was frequently visited by British aristocracy, but, by all odds, the most interesting visitors were members of the Royal Family. His Majesty, King George, dropped in on more than one occasion, just like an ordinary citizen, without the usual frills and pageantry that accompany Royalty. In his visit to St. Dunstan's he went through the place without even an equerry in attendance. He showed a deep and sincere interest in the training and work of the men. He seemed to be a little sceptical about our ability as poultry-raisers. On one occasion, when visiting the poultry-house while a class was being instructed, he signified that he would like a practical test of the power of the blind to distinguish different breeds of fowls. The attendant caught a bird and handed it to one of the students, an Imperial officer, by the way, and scarcely had he touched it [Pg 56] before he correctly pronounced it a Plymouth Rock. The King was still sceptical, and a second and third bird were handed the demonstrator, and the birds were properly named. This convinced His Majesty that, though blind, the men could "carry on" in what seemed to him an incredibly difficult occupation for the sightless.

Mat Weaving

Her Majesty, Queen Mary, took an equally active interest in our hostel. I met her under peculiar circumstances at the Bungalow. I had just entered the Lounge from the Shorthand Room, when I heard the "Skipper" calling me. I went up to him through an opening between a line of chairs. When I reached Captain McMahon, he said: "Her Majesty, Queen Mary, wishes to meet you, Rawlinson." And to the Queen he remarked: "This is Rawlinson, who is learning to be a stenographer." Her Majesty showed genuine interest in me, as she did in all the boys, and asked me many questions about my wound, the circumstances under which I received it, and what part of the line I was operating in when I was struck. She then questioned me about the progress I was mak [Pg 57] ing with my work, and about my life in the Bungalow. She finally complimented me on my ability in finding my way about despite my handicap. It is not every day that a private has the privilege of chatting familiarly with a queen, and in my vanity I answered: "I know my surroundings at St. Dunstan's as well as I do the palm of my hand." After a moment's silence, I asked Captain Mac if that was all he wanted of me. He said that would do, and I turned to depart. But while talking to the Queen I must have turned slightly without knowing it, and I had lost my bearings. I stepped out boldly, and tumbled clean over one of the chairs, and that after boasting to Her Majesty that I knew the place "as well as I do the palm of my hand." It was truly literally a case of pride going before a fall.

About half an hour later, I was going down the garden walk leading to the Outer Circle, when I heard women's voices farther down the path. I honk-honked—the usual signal of the boys when wishing the right of way. Among the party in front of me was the Matron of the House, who said to me: "Come on, Rawlinson, the way is all clear." [Pg 58]

"Is that you, Matron," I replied; then, in a simulated injured tone, I remarked that I had been talking to Queen Mary that afternoon, and: "Would you believe it, Matron, she had not the good manners to shake hands with a guy."

The Matron answered me in a somewhat flurried tone: "Her Majesty is here, Rawlinson."

Needless to say, I was somewhat abashed. Canada had gone far beyond his objective, as usual, but Canada was unfamiliar with retreat, and I determined to stand by my guns.

"Well," said I, "will she shake hands now?"

"I surely will," replied the Queen. She did it with a firm pressure that showed genuine feeling. She then asked me if I were out for a walk. "No," I replied, "I'm going to meet another queen. Two queens in one afternoon is not bad going for an old Canuck, is it?" "It certainly is not," she replied. "And I do hope," she added with a merry laugh, "that the other queen will not forget to shake hands when she meets you."

As I went away I heard her remark that [Pg 59] that is "a very cheerful boy; his blindness does not seem to trouble him much." She was right. It did not by this time. I had so far progressed with my work that the future was assured; work and happiness I could still find in this old world.

While at St. Dunstan's I had still another meeting with Royalty. One day I was walking up the Lounge, along the strip sacred to the sightless, when bump I went against someone who was stooping over while questioning another student. I had collided with a woman, who immediately turned and apologized most profusely for being in my way. She was most sorry that she "did not see me coming." I was in an irritated mood; the sightless always are under such circumstances. A collision of this sort always reminds them of their handicap, a thing they delight to ignore. Impatiently, I replied: "That's all right, ma'am. But if you people with eyes, when you visit us, would only remember that there are some men here that cannot see just as well as they once did, it would make it easier for us." Again she apologized, and took my hand, giving it such [Pg 60] a hearty, sympathetic pressure that I felt somewhat ashamed of myself for my hasty words. As I renewed my walk up the Lounge, one of the V.A.D.'s overtook me, and asked what had happened. I told her, and she almost took my breath away by telling me that I had been "saucing" Her Most Gracious Majesty, Queen Alexandra. I quite expected to be "on the carpet" before the chief for my words, for Sir Arthur was standing by, and must have heard them. But Sir Arthur had a way of avoiding causing his boys the slightest pain, and he no doubt knew that when I realized to whom I had spoken so hastily, my chagrin would be sufficient punishment. I hope the good Queen has forgiven my lack of courtesy, and forgotten the incident—a thing I am not likely to do. [Pg 61]

CHAPTER VIII

IN PLAYTIME

It was not all work at St. Dunstan's. Sports were encouraged and fostered in every way; but rowing and tug-of-war were by far the most popular. Fully sixty per cent. of the men went in for rowing, and some very skilful and powerful oarsmen were turned out. There were two regattas each year. The preliminary heats of each regatta were pulled off on the lake that runs into the grounds of the House, and the finals took place on the River Thames. Single sculls, pair-oars, and fours were our strong points. The Bungalow turned out two men who had no superiors on the river either sighted or sightless. Sergeant Barry, at one time the world's champion sculler, coached the team during the seasons of 1917 and 1918. So successful were the Canadians that there are now a number of St. Dunstan's rowing prizes in Canada. [Pg 62]

The tug-of-war team, of which I was a member, was quite as successful as the oarsmen. Indeed, we lost only one point during the whole season. We treated all comers alike: they were there to be pulled over; and we saw to it that they came. The following was our war song; we sang it going to the grounds, and we sang it coming away.

The Canucks are on the rope, on the rope, on the rope;
Their breasts are full of hope, full of hope, full of hope;
They tell the teams they pull against
That they're out to win the cup.
Canadians do your bit, do your bit, show your grit;
Lay back on that rope, legs well braced; never sit.
Make your snow-clad country proud
Of her boys who are on the line.

Chorus—

Take the strain, take the strain;
First a heave, then a pull, then again.

The boys are pulling, the boys are pulling;
[Pg 63] Yes, they're pulling with might and main.
Take the strain, take the strain;
First a heave, then a pull, then again.
They'll come over; they'll come over;
For the timber wolves are winning once again.

Not a very elaborate piece of poetry, and sadly deficient in metre and rhyme; but it certainly did mean much to us when we heard our supporters singing it. We sang it to the tune of "Over there." Out of justice to my comrades, I must plead guilty of composing it.

The average weight of the team was only 145lbs., but what the men lacked in weight was made up in grit. The team was chosen from fifteen Canadians, all who were at the Bungalow at the time; and seven of the nine men who comprised the team were "black" blind. Yet this team beat the pick of five hundred others. I have heard some of the men of the other teams asking: "Why do they always pull us over? We are heavier, man for man we are stronger, and we have more sight than they have."

One of the opponents discovered the secret, and thus expressed himself: "I know what it is; it's the—what they themselves call 'pep'; [Pg 64] it's the vim they put into the game; it's the enthusiasm they have for all sorts of sport. I was billeted close to some of them on the Somme; they were always the same whether in or out of the line."

He hit the nail on the head. The Canadians had the vim, the dogged determination; they would not submit to defeat, even in sport.

My mention of lack of sight among the men might seem superfluous to those who have not pulled on a tug-of-war team. The advantage of sight lies in the fact that a man to use his strength to the best advantage must make a straight pull. If any member of the team is pulling at an angle, those behind him are wasting their own pull while minimizing his. For success, all must pull together, and the rope must be kept straight and taut.

Theatricals did much to add pleasure to our lives. We not only enjoyed those of outside performers, but we put on several plays, and the boys took their parts well, and a prompter was very little in evidence. The sighted are at a loss to understand how a drama, comedy, or sketch can be enjoyed [Pg 65] by the sightless. But the spoken word acts on the inward eye, and the entire stage is revealed as vividly to the brain as if it were carried there by sight. One of the annoying things to a sightless person is to have some sighted friend sit by him at a play, describing costumes and scenery. The blind have no need of such aids.

Chief among our sources of amusement was the Rag-time Band, which did much to enliven our idle hours. Any who have been lucky enough to hear this band have had a rare treat. It was composed entirely of men who had been "over," and had lost their sight. But this loss of sight had not lessened their love of music or their power of musical expression, as many of the boys who were in hospital in London can testify. High-class singers, theatrical parties, in fact, all the leading theatrical performers and many minor ones, paid their tribute to the boys by entertaining them with song and sketch; but no performance had quite the same popularity as the rag-time discoursed by the "blind boys." And the remarkable thing about the band is that it is doubtful if any member had [Pg 66] ever, before going to St. Dunstan's, played a more elaborate instrument than a Jew's-harp or a mouth organ. The side-drummer, who played the side-drum, bass drum, cymbals, Chinese block, motor-horn, triangle, and clappers was a boy who had lost both eyes.

I have vivid recollections of the celebration at St. Dunstan's on Armistice Day, November 11th, 1918; on that day the band excelled itself, and played as if it meant that its music should be heard in Germany. This occasion is one that will live long in the memory of those of us who were at St. Dunstan's when the "scrap of paper" virtually ending the war was signed. Our Rag-time Band then really came into its own. Ask London. She will tell you that there was never a more popular band in the city. The students of St. Dunstan's paraded through the streets of the great metropolis in full regalia. As an initial step to our parade, we managed somehow or other to secure a disused old fire-engine, and on this the band piled. Sir Arthur's battalion lined up in fours and followed. Through the busiest streets of the city we marched with, at first, [Pg 67] about two hundred and fifty men in the parade. But before we had finished we extended over more than a quarter of a mile. A procession of munitioners happened to meet us, and when they found out who we were they immediately tacked themselves onto our little line. We marched to Buckingham Palace, and here we were halted by our leader—a Canadian, by the way. It seems that word had been passed to their Majesties that the St. Dunstan's men were outside. At any rate, they both came out, and I doubt if his Majesty ever had such a salute as was given him on that day. Sergeant-Major George Eades, a Canadian pioneer, drooped the colours with a flag that could not have measured more than a foot square; but his Majesty took the salute and answered it.

Sightless Canadian Four

Besides the amusements already mentioned, dances were held frequently and thoroughly enjoyed. Then, as I have said, there was rowing, and Regent's Park Lake was constantly visited by blind lads and their friends to enjoy this sport. We had even a four-oared Canadian crew—all blind, and as they skimmed over the lake, rowing in perfect time, an observer would have difficulty in detecting that they were sightless. [Pg 68]

CHAPTER IX

MEMORIES OF THE FIGHTING FRONT

During my early days at St. Dunstan's, I was inclined to brood a bit, and the past was constantly before my mind's eye; but gradually under occupation the past became shadowy, and the future was for me the only reality. Even the scenes through which I had passed in the months I was at the front took on the semblance of a dream—sometimes a nightmare; but it seemed to me that it was not I—the St. Dunstan's student—who had endured cold and wet and forced marches, who had felt the shock of high-explosive shells, the stinging threat of machine-gun and rifle bullets, who had taken part in wild charges over the top, but some other being. However, in the stillness of the night, one incident I had experienced, one scene I had witnessed, kept constantly recurring to my mind with a vividness that kept the World War and my humble part in it a stern reality [Pg 69] for me. The affair in question occurred on April 19th, 1917.

Ten days before, on Easter Monday—a red-letter day for the Canadians, but a day black as night for the Germans—the troops from the Dominion had in one swift forward movement swept the enemy from positions which he had thought impregnable along Vimy Ridge. For days after that, we wallowed around in the mud, gaining a village here, a trench there, and driving him from hills and wood fastnesses. All the time we were expecting that he would come back in force to make a mighty effort to regain the territory he had held for over two years against the British and the French. He had apparently proved his right to it, and since September 15th, 1916, had been resting at his ease in his underground dug-outs and capacious caverns.

On the night of the 19th, the battalion to which I belonged had just ended a tour of duty in the front line. We were to be relieved by another battalion of the 3rd Division of the Canadian Corps. There was but one road out, a road which at that time was [Pg 70] considered a masterpiece of road-building. Three days had been allotted for its construction. The Imperial engineers contended that the task was an impossible one, but G.H.Q. said it would have to be done, and the Canadian engineers were assigned the work. To their credit, it was completed in the stipulated time.

To retire from the side of the ridge facing the German position, it was necessary to take this road, and, as the crest of it was under almost continuous shell-fire, for safety we were sent over in sections of ten men at a time. This territory had all been in Fritzie's hands, and he knew every inch of it. The road was a vital spot, and more shells were dropped on it than upon any other place of the same area on the Western front. On the top, about two hundred yards away, lay the ruined village of Thelus; once in it we should be comparatively safe.

I was in the last section of my platoon, and at the top I paused to look about me at the scene that presented itself. It was horrible; it was glorious; it was magnificent—it was War. The centre of the road was [Pg 71] fairly clear, but at the edges all was chaos. The night was a wonderful one; the moon was shining in all her glory, and pale stars twinkled in the sky. In the bright moonlight I could see all about me dead and wounded men, wounded men who would surely "go West," for, once down, the chance of escape from that hell-hole was slight. Here and there were great W.D. waggons, G.S. waggons, ammunition mules bearing 6-inch howitzer and the smaller 18-pounder equipment—in fact, everything that was in any way connected with the grim business that was being carried on. Here and there, too, through this chaos of war, ration parties wended their way to and from the front line trenches.

Just as we reached the crest of the ridge, that spur of France that had taken such heavy toll from Hun and Ally, we heard a warning shout: "Keep to the edge of the road!" We wondered at the caution. The middle of the road was comparatively clean, while towards the edges it was ankle-deep in sticky mud, and we had been floundering around in a quagmire for the last eleven days. [Pg 72] But we soon knew the reason; for while we hesitated up came a battery of guns at full gallop—big howitzers at that. Drivers shouted; horses plunged and tugged at their traces; the guns bounded and rattled in and out of the shell-holes that pitted the road, sometimes seeming to be balanced on only one wheel. It was a thrilling sight, such as comes to the eyes of a man only once in a lifetime. It gripped us all. Poor Sergeant Harry Best, our platoon sergeant, who was near me, relieved the tension by exclaiming: "Get that, Jim! You will never see such a sight again, even if you stayed out here for fifty years. If a painter were to put that sight on canvas he would be laughed at as a dreamer."

I said, poor Sergeant Best! He had seen the sight of his lifetime, but he was not long to enjoy it, for the next trip in, when he was all ready to go to London to take his commission, he was "sent West" by a bomb from a trench mortar. Harry was a little strict, but he was dead fair, and, best of all, a thorough soldier. How is it that nearly all the good ones get, or seem to get, the worst of [Pg 73] the deal; they certainly play for the most part in hard luck. But then they take risks that the "safety-first" soldier never takes. [Pg 74]

CHAPTER X

THE POINT OF VIEW OF THE SIGHTLESS

When I began to write this personal narrative I had two main thoughts in mind. My first was that no work written on the World War would be complete without some account of the transference of the soldier back from khaki to mufti; my second, and to my mind the more important, was to show the man himself, suffering from a serious handicap, that one of the greatest truths in this life of ours is: there is nothing that a man cannot do, if he *has* to. This needs explanation. There are few men who have come out of this war just as they went into it. Apart from injuries they have sustained, there is unavoidably a new outlook upon life, gained by their sojourn in the trenches. No matter who the man is, no matter how settled were his views on the management of this old world, his stay "over there" has changed his point of view. His whole mental attitude has undergone [Pg 75] something of the nature of a revolution in the crucible of war. Up the "line," he saw things stripped to the buff, saw life and death in all their nakedness. The veneer of so-called civilization has been worn off, and the *real man* shows through. That, to my mind, is why friendships made amid the blood, mud, hunger, and grime of the trenches are friendships that will endure through life. It is there *Man* meets *Man*, and admires him. I have met men in the trenches to whom, had I met them in ordinary life, I would not have given a second thought. When they first came to the front they were known as "sissies," but not for long. They, for the most part, quickly acquired that character and bearing that is the rule of the trenches. There were exceptions, of course, but not many. As I write there comes to my mind a little incident that happened in a dug-out in a trench known to the 9th Brigade as Mill Street. Those who were there at the time will remember it from the fact that the body of a French soldier was lying half buried under the parapet at one of the entrances. Poor Frenchy's whole right side was [Pg 76] showing from the foot to the waist line. The day of which I write had been rather warm. A working party had been out repairing a firing step and revetting the trench. A "sissy" came down the steps of the dug-out, mopping his forehead with a handkerchief;—fancy any one carrying a handkerchief in the front line; one had essentials enough to carry without being burdened with such a feminine article;—another of the boys was sitting writing a letter with his ground-sheet under him in the mud. The sissified one blurted out: "Holy gee! but I'm perspiring profusely." The kid writing the letter looked up and sarcastically answered, "Wouldn't sweatin' like 'ell be more to the point." Later in my military career I had a chat with the commander of the company to which the "sissy" belonged, and he incidentally remarked that the lad had turned out to be one of the most reliable and plucky fellows in the battalion. I have often wondered since if that little remark "sweatin' like hell" had not helped him to buck up and fit into his general surroundings.

Since I have been sightless, two things have [Pg 77] deeply impressed themselves on my mind. The first is that no person with sight can, or ever will be able to, see from a blind man's point of view; the second, that no one who can see can ever understand or gauge a blind man's capabilities or limitations. When I speak of a blind man in this sketch, I, of course, refer to those who have suddenly been deprived of sight. Of the man who was born blind or who became sightless early in life I do not profess to know anything. But the viewpoint of the blind is, in the majority of cases, different from that of the sighted—I mean in the matter of earning one's living and making oneself independent of charity. The man who has been blinded in battle has seen life—and death for that matter—stripped of all its frills and flounces. His mind and viewpoint have been enlarged and broadened by his life in the Army. But he sees life from an angle that is denied the sighted. To be made into a wage-earner he must be handled rightly. He must not be "mollycoddled"; to do so would be to leave him a burden to himself and to his friends. He must not be made to feel that he is an object [Pg 78] to be set in a corner where he can hurt neither himself nor others. It does not do to treat blind men in the lump; they must be handled individually. Each and every case stands by itself. Tact, and a lot of it, patience, and perseverance are the essentials for remaking a man who has lost his sight, into what he desires to be—a being capable of earning a living and producing results in the industrial world. For the attainment of this end, two things are necessary — confidence and independence. Once he has learned these, he has won half his battle — a hard battle, how hard he alone realizes. For my own part, my first two months of blindness, at least, were Hell with a capital H. Let me illustrate what I mean by confidence and independence.

Whilst at St. Dunstan's, I was, for some reason or other, given the job on quite a few occasions of meeting men who were feeling rather harder than was thought necessary the darkness that enveloped them. If a man came in feeling that there was nothing in life for him now that he was blind, I was given the task of cheering him up and showing him, if I could — and I have the satisfaction of know [Pg 79] ing that I did not often fail — that this old world was not such a bad place, even if one's lights were put out. One case stands out with prominence, and when I look back at the results of my work after twelve months have passed, it is not without a measure of pride.

One Saturday afternoon, a young Canadian came to the Bungalow. He was talked to by both the Adjutant and the Matron, who did all in their power to "buck" him up. They failed hopelessly, as the "kid" felt too far gone; he just would not try to look at the bright side of life. Then some one suggested that he be brought over to "Rawly." When we met, I began our conversation with: "Well, kid, how are things?" He snapped back: "For God's sake, another preacher!" It was somewhat of a staggerer, but I had been through it all myself, and understood the boy's feelings perfectly. In the darkness that sealed his eyes he was forced to grope his way about stumblingly, usually with the help of a guide. He had not yet gained confidence in his own powers. I straightway determined to inspire him with that confidence.

In the first days of my sojourn at St. [Pg 80] Dunstan's, I, for a time, felt that never again should I be able to step out into the world except with halting step and a horror of what might happen. The management of the institution had constructed an elaborate system of gravel paths, along which were wooden palings which would prevent the students losing their way. A knob in these palings told of a turning; a plank served to warn that we were approaching steps or a steep incline. In the work-rooms and through out the entire buildings, strips of carpet served as a guide to the feet. But it took time to gain confidence even with these aids; and then they were confined to the buildings and grounds. Confidence would only come when one was able to navigate his way alone through busy thoroughfares. Shortly after entering St. Dunstan's I determined to venture out alone. A guide accompanied me on my outward journey, but I dismissed him and determined to find my way back without help. I cautiously kept to the outside of the walk, using my stick as a guide, but I had not calculated on obstructing posts; bump I went into one, but nothing daunted, I kept [Pg 81] on. I was about to test the hardness of another with my head when a sympathetic soul seized me by the arm and saved me just in time. I asked him to direct me to the wall bordering the walk. He did so; but I had not taken into consideration the fact that there were stores with goods out for display in front of them. I was first made aware of this by hitting a somewhat flimsily-constructed fruit stand. At this moment a motorcycle a few feet away back-fired viciously. It sounded like the explosion of a shell. Vimy and its horrors came back on the instant, and I involuntarily ducked for safety, or, rather, sprawled forward at full length. Down came the fruit stand, and there I lay among apples, oranges, and bananas. Kindly hands helped me to my feet, and set me on my way. My first experience of solitary walking out had been a rough one, and for a time I felt beaten, and had very much the attitude of this boy towards the future. But my experiences would help him. I had conquered in time, and could journey about freely without even the aid of a stick. I would not let him know that [Pg 82] I was "black" blind, but I would take him out with me and show him what the blind could do unaided if they would only bring into play their latent powers.

We chatted for a time about the war, and the prospect of his return to Canada and his friends. He gradually thawed out, and took me in a measure into his confidence. But he was still in the depths, and continually referred to his deplorable lot. There was, he said, nothing in this world for him now, and he added pathetically: "I'm only twenty years old; I have seen practically nothing, and as both my eyes are out, I never shall be able to enjoy life and nature. I wish I had got the full issue instead of half of it; I should have been a lot better off."

Now, there is an unfailing means to get on the good side of any one who has spent any time in "Blighty," and that is to suggest tea. So I asked him if he would not like a cup and some cake: I knew, I said, a nice tea-room where we could get a good cup.

"Yes," he replied, "I should enjoy something to drink; but who will take me to your tea-room?" [Pg 83]

"Come with me," I said; "I will be your pilot."

So away we toddled out of the Bungalow and down the rails which run round the Outer Circle, right through Clarence Gate, down Upper Baker Street, past the Tube, and across the road to Gentle's. Well, we had the tea; and companionship and the refreshments seemed to cheer up the lad. At any rate, he began to talk about things they told him he could learn at St. Dunstan's; and I seized the opportunity to say: "Well, things are not quite as bad as they seemed at first, eh? You see we got down here all right." This was in answer to his saying that one would always be compelled to depend on a guide in his ramblings.

"Yes," he replied, "we got here all right, but you can see some. It's easy for you guys to talk about getting around by yourselves when you can see, be it never so dimly; but remember that I have both my eyes out."

This was what I had been working for and waiting for all afternoon. I wanted him to think that I could see; my turn would come sooner or later, and my answer to him would make him buck up if anything could. [Pg 84]

"Eh, old boy," I said, with a degree of exultation; "I am as 'black' blind as you are. I have one eye, it is true, but it is na-poo, finis, just as much as your's are."

"Do you really mean that, Jim?" he asked.

"I certainly do; and you just fell into the bear-pit I had ready for you."

"Well, let me tell you," he said, with stern determination, "if you have done this, here's another boy who can do likewise."

That boy returned to Canada with a full knowledge of poultry-breeding and egg-producing, basket-making, rough carpentry, and all kinds of string work, such as hammock and net weaving. He became one of the brightest and happiest students in St. Dunstan's, and, incidentally, I might mention that that same lad, who felt himself down and out for all time, developed into one of the best dancers that ever put foot in slipper.

Basket Making

Another lad—an Australian, this time—wanted to go over the House. I acted as his pilot, and on our way back to the Bungalow he asked me how much I could see. I told him, "nothing." He answered: "Say, Digger, I've been taking some chances, haven't I? But [Pg 85] this I will tell you, the next time I want to come over here I am going to find the way myself."

All that those boys needed was to realize that others who were handicapped as they were could work and move about on their own initiative, and they would be quick to follow their example. Confidence is infectious; it passes from one individual to another. Above all, it is the absolute foundation for success in a man who cannot see — or, for that part of it, in any man.

I have said sufficient to show that the man from whom the external world is suddenly shut out is still able to "carry on." For my own part, I have returned to Canada, and am busy in useful employment, working among comrades similarly situated with myself. Three years ago, had any one told me that a blind man could qualify as a stenographer I should have ridiculed the idea. But I am now able to take dictation in Braille shorthand at the rate of one hundred and twenty words per minute and then transcribe my notes on any typewriting machine on the market just as speedily as the ordinary sighted typist. And I never operated a typewriting [Pg 86] machine before I became a student at St. Dunstan's.

As I said, I am back in Canada, and not getting my living through charity. What I am I owe to St. Dunstan's, and while labouring here my heart ever goes back to dear old England. I feel towards St. Dunstan's—and so do all the boys who have passed through her halls—as does the grown man for the place of his birth. She is home for me. I was born again and nurtured into a new manhood by her, led by her from stygian darkness to mental and spiritual light, and my heart turns with longing towards her. At times, separation from the genial atmosphere of this paradise of the sightless, from contact with the dominating, kindly presence of Sir Arthur Pearson and his noble assistants, weighs heavily upon my spirits. But there is work to be done here in Canada, and, in a humble way, I am able to continue the good work done at St. Dunstan's; if not in a militant way, at least by example, taking my place among the producers, toiling daily with hands and brain. [Pg 87]